Following the Rules

I know rules are good for me.

I can show respect.

I look at others when they talk to me.

I take good care of property.

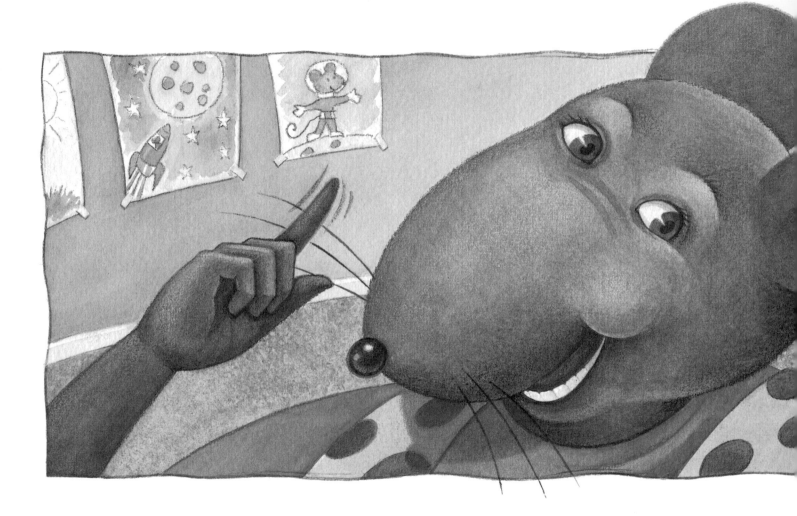

I know rules are good for me.

I can show respect.

I'm fair to others when I play games.

And I never call people names.

I know rules are good for me. I can show respect.

I always wait my turn in line.

I obey the rules and all the signs.

I know rules are good for me. I can show respect.

I mind my teachers and my parents every day.

I'm careful about the things I say.

I know rules are good for me. I can show respect.